FAIRY SPELL

How Two Girls Convinced the World That Fairies Are Real

MARC TYLER NOBLEMAN

Illustrated by ELIZA WHEELER

CLARION BOOKS
Houghton Mifflin Harcourt | Boston New York

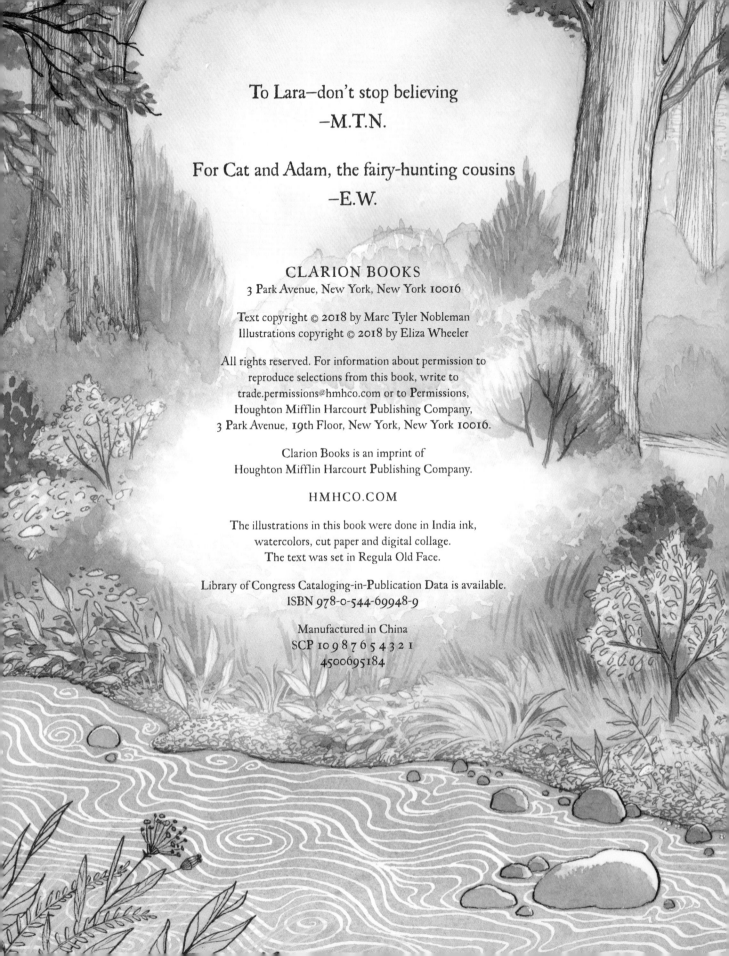

To Lara—don't stop believing
—M.T.N.

For Cat and Adam, the fairy-hunting cousins
—E.W.

CLARION BOOKS
3 Park Avenue, New York, New York 10016

Text copyright © 2018 by Marc Tyler Nobleman
Illustrations copyright © 2018 by Eliza Wheeler

Clarion Books is an imprint of
Houghton Mifflin Harcourt Publishing Company.

HMHCO.COM

The illustrations in this book were done in India ink,
watercolors, cut paper and digital collage.
The text was set in Regula Old Face.

Library of Congress Cataloging-in-Publication Data is available.
ISBN 978-0-544-69948-9

Manufactured in China
SCP 10 9 8 7 6 5 4 3 2 1
4500695184

ET AGAIN, nine-year-old Frances Griffiths had fallen into the water.

Her expensive shoes were soaking wet.

Her mother was furious.

Her aunt **P**olly asked, "Why do you keep going to the beck?"

Frances paused. "To see the fairies."

Fairies? "Nonsense," said her uncle Arthur.

1917

Annie & Frances Griffiths

Frances and her mother
had moved from South Africa
to Cottingley, England, while
Frances's father was serving
in World War I.

Sgt. Griffiths

They were staying
with the Wrights—
her aunt, uncle, and
sixteen-year-old cousin,
Elsie. Frances and Elsie,
both only children, had
become like sisters.

Polly, Elsie & Arthur Wright

Elsie & Frances

The Wright home sat on the highest point
in the village. Behind it stretched a garden,
and burbling at the bottom of the garden was
the beck, or stream.

Throughout the summer of 1917, the beck had called to Frances and Elsie, and they spent many happy hours there. Though it was mere yards from the house, they sometimes brought lunch so they wouldn't have to leave for any longer than necessary.

But that day, Frances was on the verge of tears because the adults did not believe her fairy tale. Elsie said to her father, "If you'll let me have your camera and tell me how it works, I'll get a photo of the fairies."

Photography was new enough that many people had never taken a picture. Cameras could be complicated to use. Arthur said no.

The girls pleaded with him for days. One July afternoon he finally agreed. He supplied them with one plate—meaning they could take only one picture. Less than an hour later, they reappeared with knowing smiles.

"We've got the photo, I believe," Elsie said.
"Will you look?"

She squeezed into their small darkroom with
her father while Frances waited outside.

Arthur began to develop the photo. As the image
took shape, he thought he was looking at birds
or sandwich wrappers until he saw legs . . .
and arms. Tiny ones.

"The fairies are on the plate!" Elsie shouted to
Frances, who squealed and danced on the other
side of the door.

Arthur was speechless. Then he laughed. He felt Frances and Elsie were playing a joke. But the girls swore they did only as they said they would: prove that fairies frolicked at the beck.

"If anybody else were there, the fairies would not come out," Elsie said. "The fairies would not come out for you in a hundred years." The adults could not figure out how—or if—they were being fooled.

In September, Arthur again loaned Frances and Elsie his camera. Again the girls scurried to the beck for a short while. And again they scrambled back with a photo the adults could not believe: Elsie holding hands with a gnome.

This time, Arthur was more annoyed than amused. The girls still would not confess, so Arthur forbade them from using his camera. But Polly had quietly begun to feel that, somehow, the girls were telling the truth.

On November 9, 1918, Frances sent a friend in South Africa a letter and enclosed one of the fairy photographs. On the back of the photo she wrote: "Elsie and I are very friendly with the beck Fairies. It is funny I never used to see them in Africa. It must be too hot for them there."

Novem...
Dear J...
I hop...
letter before...

Elsie and I are very friendly with the beck Fairies. It is funny I never used to see them in Africa. It must be too hot for them there.

nave made h...
Rosebud

Two days later, World War I ended.
Frances's father returned and the
Griffiths family moved to Scarborough,
a town about two hours from Cottingley.

The following summer, the girls' mothers attended a lecture on fairies. Polly showed the speaker the photos Frances and Elsie had taken and asked, "Are fairies really true?"

News of the photos spread to Edward Gardner, a man well known for speaking on topics of the supernatural, and then to Arthur Conan Doyle, the author who created the world-famous detective Sherlock Holmes.

EDWARD GARDNER

ARTHUR CONAN DOYLE

Conan Doyle was no stranger to the possibility of fairies; his father said he often saw them. Intrigued, Gardner and Conan Doyle decided to investigate the photos together. For Conan Doyle, the timing was apt—he had already been preparing to write about fairies for *The Strand*, a popular British magazine.

Gardner visited the Wrights in Cottingley. He said that Conan Doyle would like to publish the photos with his article. Although Elsie and her parents turned him down at first, they eventually agreed, so long as the magazine did not print their real names or identify their village.

Gardner asked Harold Snelling, a photographer with thirty years of experience, to examine the photos. Snelling said, "This is the most extraordinary thing I've ever seen!" In fact, Snelling believed that while the photo was being taken, the fairies had *moved*.

If they moved, they must be real. And if the girls had taken two photos, they could take more.

Frances was sent to Cottingley so the girls
could go out to the beck to summon—or "'tice,"
as they said—the fairies.

But it rained . . . every day. In the two weeks
Frances was in Cottingley, the girls got only two
hours of sunshine to try for photos.

The girls' first two photos appeared in the December 1920 issue of *The Strand*. The magazine called them

THE TWO MOST ASTOUNDING PHOTOGRAPHS EVER PUBLISHED.

In Conan Doyle's article, Frances was "Alice" and Elsie was "Iris." So while the girls kept their privacy, their nameless friends from the beck were introduced to the public.

The issue sold out in three days.

IRIS AND THE DANCING GNOME.

(An undouched enlargement from the original negative.)

THIS PICTURE AND THE EVEN MORE EXTRAORDINARY
ONE OF THE FAIRIES ON PAGE 465 ARE THE TWO
MOST ASTOUNDING PHOTOGRAPHS EVER PUBLISHED.
HOW THEY WERE TAKEN IS FULLY DESCRIBED IN SIR
A. CONAN DOYLE'S AMAZING ARTICLE.

(See page 466.)

Fairies Photographed

AN EPOCH-MAKING EVENT .... DESCRIBED BY A. CONAN DOYLE

SHOULD the incidents here narrated, and the photographs attached, hold their own against the criticism which they will excite, it is no exaggeration to say that they will mark an epoch in human thought. I put them and all the evidence before the public for examination and judgment. If I am myself asked whether I consider the case to be absolutely and finally proved, I should answer that in order to remove the last faint shadow of doubt I should wish to see the result repeated before a disinterested witness. At the same time, I recognize the difficulty of such a request, since rare results must be obtained when and how they can. But short of final and absolute proof, I consider, after carefully going into every possible source of error, that a strong *prima facie* case has been built up. The cry of "fake" is sure to be raised, and will make some impression upon those who have not had the opportunity of knowing the people concerned, or the place. On the photographic side every objection has been considered and adequately met. The pictures stand or fall together. Both are false, or both are true. All the circumstances point to the latter alternative, and yet in a matter involving so tremendous a new departure one needs overpowering evidence before one can say that there is no conceivable loophole for error.

It was about the month of May in this year that I received a letter from Miss Felicia Scatcherd, so well known in several departments of human thought, to the effect that two photographs of fairies had been taken in the North of England under circumstances which seemed to put fraud out of the question. The statement would have

appealed to me at any time, but I happened at the moment to be collecting material for an article on fairies, now completed, and I had accumulated a surprising number of cases of people who claimed to be able to see these little creatures. The evidence was so complete and detailed, with such good names attached to it, that it was difficult to believe that it was false; but, being by nature of a somewhat sceptical turn, I felt that something closer was needed before I could feel personal conviction and assure myself that these were not thought-forms conjured up by the imagination or expectation of the seers. The rumour of the photographs interested me deeply, therefore, and following the matter up from one lady informant to another, I came at last upon Mr. Edward L. Gardner, who has been ever since my most efficient collaborator, to whom all credit is due. Mr. Gardner, it may be remarked, is a member of the Executive Committee of the Theosophical Society, and a well-known lecturer upon occult subjects.

He had not himself at that time mastered the whole case, but all he had he placed freely at my disposal. I had already seen prints of the photographs, but I was relieved to find that he had the actual negatives, and that it was from them, and not from the prints, that two expert photographers, especially Mr. Snelling, of 26, The Bridge, Wealdstone, Harrow, had already formed their conclusions in favour of the genuineness of the pictures. Mr. Gardner tells his own story presently, so I will simply say that at that period he had got into direct and friendly touch with the Carpenter family. We are compelled to use a pseudonym and to with-

Vol. lx.—31

Everyone was aflutter about the fairy photos. While some readers thought the girls had made a historic discovery, others thought the photos were fake—and couldn't grasp how a smart man like Arthur Conan Doyle could believe they were real.

Some doubters pointed out that the waterfall behind
Frances was blurry but the fairies were not; if both
the water and the fairies were moving, *both* should be
blurry. Others questioned why Frances was looking at
the camera rather than the fanciful fairies.

Conan Doyle said the wings were not blurred because a fairy
is a combination of human and butterfly whose body doesn't
work like those of either humans or butterflies.

Gardner said Frances was not looking at the fairies because she was used to them; what she was *not* used to was the camera. But the main reason the two men felt the photos were truthful was because the two girls came from decent families and had no history of hoaxing.

A few months later, under the headline "The Evidence for Fairies," *The Strand* ran Frances and Elsie's last three photos.

A reporter found out that Alice and Iris were really Frances and Elsie. The attention soon became so overwhelming that the girls were eager to say farewell to fairies. Besides, they were growing up.

Elsie married in 1926, Frances in 1928. They had children, got jobs, and settled in different parts of England.

People stopped bothering them . . . until 1965.

A journalist tracked down
Elsie, then sixty-four years old.
The fairy photo frenzy started all
over again.

"Let's say they are figments of our imaginations, Frances's and mine, and leave it at that," Elise said. Some people took that to mean that the girls made up the fairies. Others thought that clever Elsie was not admitting anything one way or the other.

"What did you say that for?" Frances, then fifty-eight years old, wrote in a letter to Elsie. "You know very well they were real."

In 1976, a TV show filmed Frances and Elsie returning to Cottingley together for the first time since the 1920s. They did not see fairies. Possibly, they said, only children can.

The next year, an author named Fred Gettings was doing research for a book he was writing about old illustrations.

Looking through *Princess Mary's Gift Book,* which had
been published in 1914, he was startled by what he saw on
page 104: a drawing of fairies accompanying a poem called
"A Spell for a Fairy."

Those fairies looked almost
identical to the ones in Frances and Elsie's first photo.

But it wasn't till six years later that the puzzle of the Cottingley fairies was solved . . . mostly. In 1983, when Elsie was eighty-one and Frances was seventy-five, Elsie revealed that they had indeed faked the photos.

Elsie had wanted to get back at the adults for scolding Frances when she came home drenched. Because Frances was younger, she went along with Elsie's plan.

shall hear a bugle calling,
Wildly over the dew-dashed down,
And a sound as of the falling
Ramparts of a conquered town.

You shall hear a sound like thunder,
And a veil shall be withdrawn,
When her eyes grow wide with wonder,
On that hill-top, in that dawn.

Elsie copied fairies from *Princess Mary's Gift Book* onto stiff paper and cut them out.

The girls attached long pins to the backs
of the drawings and stuck them into the ground
or to branches. After they snapped the photos,
they ripped up the cutouts and scattered
the pieces in the beck. (All those years
earlier, Arthur had looked for but failed
to find such scraps.)

Neither girl could have had any
idea that a backyard prank on their
parents would blow up into a
front-page prank on
the world.

"I can't understand why people were taken in," Frances said. "They *wanted* to be taken in."

Frances and Elsie kept the secret almost their whole lives. Even their parents had never learned what they'd done. Part of the reason the girls did not want to divulge the truth earlier was to spare Conan Doyle and Gardner any embarrassment. But by 1983, both had passed away.

However, while Frances admitted the first four photos were frauds, she disagreed with Elsie about the last, the photo of the fairy sun-bath. Frances insisted it was the world's first photo of actual fairies.

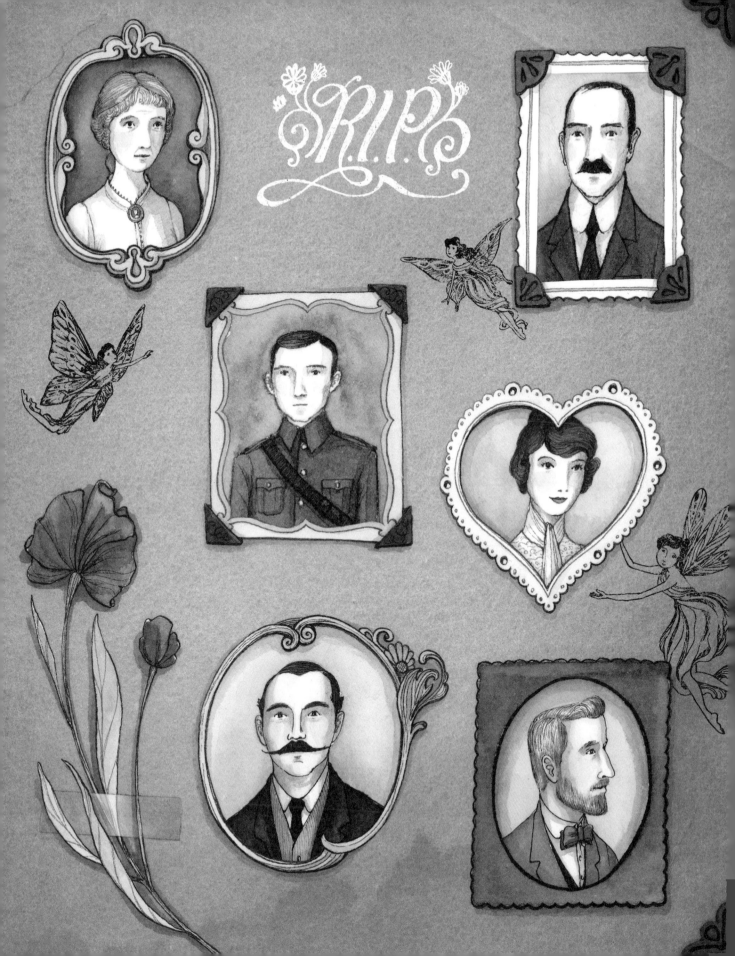

Frances was not especially concerned with whether or not people believed that the photo was real. Shortly before she died, she made clear what she most wanted people to know, to remember, to believe: "There *were* fairies at Cottingley."

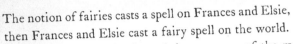

The notion of fairies casts a spell on Frances and Elsie, then Frances and Elsie cast a fairy spell on the world.

The first photo Elsie took became one of the most reproduced photos in history. Frances and the four fairies went viral . . . ninety years before social media. This was also before the average person would think about taking—let alone faking—a photo.

By the time Frances and Elsie picked up a camera, amateur photography had been around for decades. So had trick photography, or photo manipulation. After Abraham Lincoln died in 1865, people faked photos not only of the president's body in a casket but also his ghost!

Today we are more sophisticated when it comes to recognizing doctored photos, but we can still be fooled. What happened in Cottingley is not a story of the public being hoodwinked because they were simpler people in simpler times—some in 1920 dismissed the photos as frauds. Rather it is a reminder that people who want to believe *do* believe, no matter when.

The difference now is that we are trained not to accept automatically but rather to question, and when possible, to investigate on our own to determine the truth. Though the internet is a powerful tool in trying to confirm or deny a suspicious story or photo, it can also spread misinformation just as easily. Having the internet doesn't mean you can kick back and think less. On the contrary, it forces you to think more.

When I began to research the Cottingley fairies, I wondered if people would question why I wanted to write a true story for kids in which the main characters were liars. That's not how I saw them. Yes, Frances and Elsie played a trick on their parents. The girls probably thought that trick would serve its small purpose and be forgotten. They did not imagine other people—important people—would learn of the photos.

Just as their cutout fairies were stuck in the ground with pins, Frances and Elsie felt stuck in their fairy story. They wouldn't change it less because they feared being labeled as liars but more so because they didn't want to make others feel bad for believing. I loved them for that.

And it wasn't all a trick. Frances never wavered in her belief. She claimed the fairies appear only in summer and only on sunny days. They didn't talk to the girls or to one another. They didn't even seem to notice the girls. They were there doing whatever fairies do. "It was a happy time up the beck," Frances said, "with always the sound of water running over the stones and glimpses of fairies."

What do *you* believe?

SOURCES

BOOKS

Conan Doyle, Arthur. *The Coming of the Fairies.* London: Pavilion Books, 1997. First published 1922 by Hodder and Stoughton.

Cooper, Joe. *The Case of the Cottingley Fairies.* London: Robert Hale, 1990.

Gardner, Edward L. *Fairies: The Cottingley Photographs and Their Sequel.* 4th ed. London: Theosophical Publishing House, 1966. First published 1945 by Theosophical Publishing House.

Griffiths, Frances, and Christine Lynch. *Reflections on the Cottingley Fairies: Frances Griffiths—In Her Own Words* (with additional material by her daughter Christine). Belfast: JMJ Publications (self-published), 2009.

Hodson, Geoffrey. *Fairies at Work and at Play.* With an introduction by E. L. Gardner. London: Theosophical Publishing House, 1925.

Randi, James. *Flim-Flam!: Psychics, ESP, Unicorns, and Other Delusions.* Buffalo: Prometheus Books, 1982.

OTHER

Arthur C. Clarke's World of Strange Powers. "Fairies, Phantoms and Fantastic Photographs," first broadcast 22 May 1985 by ITV. Directed by Charles Flynn and produced by Yorkshire Television.

Sanderson, S. F. "The Cottingley Fairy Photographs: A Re-Appraisal of the Evidence." *Folklore* 84, no. 2 (Summer 1973): pp. 89–103.

ONLINE

Cottingley Connect. "Cottingley Fairies." www.cottingleyconnect.org.uk/fairies.shtml.

Cottingley Network. "Cottingley Fairies." www.cottingley.net/fairies.shtml.

Taylor, Troy. "Sir Arthur Conan Doyle and the 'Cottingley Fairies' Case." American Haunting. www.prairieghosts.com/fairies.html.

Some information comes from e-mail exchanges with Frances's daughter, Christine, and Elsie's son, Glenn.

All dialogue is excerpted from published or televised interviews.